The New Zealand
Gluten Free
Cookbook

Sophie Johnson

THE CAXTON PRESS

Dedication

For my Dad
Ian Johnson
20 January 1952 - 20 March 2001

© Sophie Johnson, 2009

sophiejohnson@gmx.com

ISBN 978-1-877303-15-9

Distributed by
the publishers, the author,
and Nationwide Book Distributors Ltd
PO Box 65, 351 Kiri Kiri Road, Oxford, New Zealand
www.nationwidebooks.co.nz

Published by and printed at

THE CAXTON PRESS
113 Victoria Street, PO Box 25-088
Christchurch, New Zealand
www.caxton.co.nz

Contents

Foreword

It can be daunting when you are first diagnosed with Coeliac Disease and one of the first questions a Coeliac asks is "What can I eat?" And then the fun starts.

Learning about ingredients, products and recipes that are safe for a Coeliac to eat is part of the education required to embark on the only known treatment for Coeliac disease – a life-long gluten free diet.

When Sophie sent in her recipe book for us to review we were impressed with the detail, variety and presentation of the many recipes she had compiled for the book and commend her on the initiative.

The New Zealand Gluten Free Cookbook is a recommended resource for Coeliacs or those wishing to eat gluten free.

Gill Keuskamp
President
Coeliac New Zealand

www.coeliac.co.nz

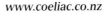

Introduction

Shortly before this book went to print, Sophie was informed by her doctor that she likely suffered from Coeliac Disease herself, following years of undiagnosed symptoms.

Welcome to all those with Coeliac Disease, the Gluten Intolerant, the voluntarily Gluten Free and their family and friends who need to cook without using gluten.

My house is a happily Gluten Free home. My partner was diagnosed with Coeliac Disease in 2005 and I find it easier to have all the food in our house Gluten Free.

You should never have to make separate meals for members of your family who are Gluten Free. I can give you meal ideas the whole family will love and they won't even know that it is Gluten Free.

The main problem for the newly Gluten Free is realising which things they eat have gluten, and that sometimes it is in the most random things that you'd never suspect.

I didn't want my partner to miss out on yummy food and I didn't want to feel guilty enjoying burgers and cakes around him. For me, the best solution was to figure out how to make everything we loved eating, Gluten Free.

It took a lot of experimentation and a lot of willing testers as well as helpful advice from gluten eaters and non-gluten eaters alike. I researched ingredients online almost every day and spend hours reading cookbooks cover to cover. Along the way I discovered new ingredients that I never would have cooked with before such as quinoa and hulled millet.

I know that in this day and age a lot of families are so busy that they'd rather grab packaged food from the supermarket than make things from scratch, but more recently the trend is to grow your own vegetables and herbs, try new foods and make food from scratch so you know exactly what's going into it. We are now more conscious of preservatives and 'fillers' and we want to eat less processed food.

I don't have anything with gluten in it in the pantry because I no longer need it. I make Gluten Free food for everyone I know regardless of whether they can eat gluten or not. I enjoy having dinner parties, making fresh pasta on the weekends and inventing and testing new Gluten Free recipes. When they work out; that makes me happy, when they don't, I take it as a challenge to make it work better no matter how many times I have to alter the recipe and test it again.

When I meet someone who has recently discovered they can't eat gluten and they're worried about what they can eat and whether they'll ever get to eat nice food again, I'm happy to tell them they don't need to worry. More and more people are becoming conscious of catering for Gluten Free people, restaurants are labelling Gluten Free meals on their menus, the supermarkets are stocking more products as they arrive on the market and you can make great tasting Gluten Free food at home.

I hope from reading this cookbook you can see how varied a Gluten Free diet can be, and have some fun in the process.

Tips

- Keep your pantry, fridge and cupboards clean, tidy and well organized.

- Plan your week's meals and buy what you need in one big weekly shop; including replacing items from your pantry that you've used during the week.

- Always shop using a shopping list and a budget and try to stick to it.

- Buy as much of your baking supplies as you can from somewhere like Bin Inn that caters for your gluten free requirements.

- Kitchen tools and equipment are helpful and I think you can never have too many of them. I can't do without my food processor, electric hand mixer, electric fry-pan, bread-maker, rice cooker, pasta machine, sandwich grill, digital scales and my large pasta pot. I also find having a wide variety of mixing bowls, platters, pots, cake tins, baking dishes, casserole dishes and good quality knives helpful.

- Always line your tins and oven trays with baking paper.

- Keep a close eye on your gluten free baking while it is in the oven as cooking times often vary.

- Many products are gluten free but not advertised as such, so it pays to always read the ingredients. You should check items even if you use them regularly to make sure the ingredients have not changed and you should check all brands on the shelf as the same product in one brand may contain gluten and in another brand be gluten free.

- I have not listed specific brands in this book as manufacturers can change ingredients at any time and I cannot guarantee the ongoing gluten-free nature or availability of individual brands.

- If you have any questions or are unsure of something consult The Coeliac Society of New Zealand (Inc).

Email : coeliac@xtra.co.nz   Website : www.coeliac.co.nz

Light Meals

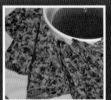 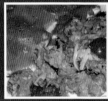  

Corn, Cheese Fritters

MAKES 15-20 PIKELET SIZED FRITTERS

INGREDIENTS

2 eggs
1½ cups pea flour
¼ cup parmesan
½ cup edam cheese
¼ cup extra light olive oil
410g can GF cream style corn
GF sweet chilli sauce
black pepper
sea salt

Mix cream style corn, pepper, eggs, parmesan, edam cheese and pea flour together in a large bowl.

If the mixture seems too runny you can add more pea flour, make sure all the flour is mixed in before making the fritters.

Heat an electric fry-pan and pour in half the olive oil.

Fry fritters until they are slightly browned and can be flipped over, continue with the remaining butter and oil.

Cook the fritters until they're as brown as you'd like them.

Serve with sweet chilli sauce and sea salt.

Spinach and Pumpkin Fritters

MAKES 15-20 PIKELET SIZED FRITTERS

Boil the spinach and pumpkin until soft.

Mash the pumpkin and spinach together in a large bowl.

Add the pea flour and mix well until all the lumps are gone.

If the mixture seems too runny you can add more pea flour.

Heat an electric fry-pan and pour in half the olive oil.

Fry fritters until they are slightly browned and can be flipped over.

Using the remaining olive oil, cook the rest of the fritters until they're as brown as you'd like them.

Serve with sweet chilli sauce and sea salt.

INGREDIENTS

650g pumpkin
160g spinach
1½ cups pea flour
½ cup extra light olive oil
GF sweet chilli sauce
sea salt

Mexican Bean Pies

MAKES 18

INGREDIENTS

1 cup frozen corn
400g can GF chilli beans or mixed beans
400g can GF mexican style tomatoes
roughly 200g GF corn chips
1 cup grated edam cheese
2 avocados diced
sour cream to serve

Preheat oven to 180°.

Cut out squares of baking paper roughly 15 x 15 cm and push into each hole of a medium muffin pan.

Soak corn chips in warm water until they turn to mush, drain and squeeze the water out with a sieve and a metal spoon.

Spoon the mushy chips into the muffin holes.

Use the back of the spoon to push the corn chips against the side of the muffin holes and mould them into cup shapes, making sure there are no gaps.

Bake for 20 minutes or more to dry out the cups until the bases are crispy.

While they are cooking mix beans, tomatoes and corn.

Grate the cheese and dice the avocado and set aside.

When the cups are dried out and crispy, leave them in the muffin pan and fill the cavities with the bean mixture and sprinkle cheese over them.

Bake for 20-25 minutes or until the cheese is browned.

Remove from the oven and leave to cool in the tin, they will have to be left to cool until they are just warm in the centre so the outside shells have time to harden.

Serve with diced avocado and sour cream on top.

Cajun Potatoes

SERVES 4

Preheat oven to 230°.

Do not peel the potatoes, wash them then chop into small cubes roughly 2cm.

Put all the potatoes into a well oiled medium sized roasting pan.

In a bowl combine maize cornflour and cajun mix.

Sprinkle all the cornflour and cajun mix evenly over the potatoes then stir through.

Sprinkle the onion flakes and garlic salt over the potatoes and pour more oil over the top then place in the oven.

Bake for 45-50 minutes stirring and turning at least twice to avoid them sticking.

Serve with plain unsweetened yoghurt or sour cream.

INGREDIENTS

½ cup maize cornflour

3 tablespoons GF cajun mix – medium hot

1 tablespoon dried onion flakes

2 teaspoons garlic salt

8 potatoes chopped into small cubes

extra light olive oil

GF plain unsweetened yoghurt or sour cream to serve

Cube Potatoes

SERVES 4

INGREDIENTS

2 teaspoons garlic salt

2 teaspoons mixed herbs

3 teaspoons dried onion flakes

1 GF chicken stock cube

1 cup boiling water

250g light sour cream

8 medium size potatoes

extra light olive oil

Wash potatoes, do not peel then chop into cubes about 2cm.

Generously oil roasting pan and fill with diced potatoes.

Sprinkle over mixed herbs, garlic salt and onion flakes.

Dissolve stock cube in boiling water and pour over potatoes.

Cook at 230° for 50 minutes stirring and turning three times.

Serve with light sour cream.

Cheesy Courgettes

SERVES 2

Preheat oven to 200°.

Slice courgettes in half lengthways.

Place the halves in a row in a shallow glass rectangular dish.

Sprinkle the cheese over the top.

Bake for 30 to 40 minutes until the cheese is just starting to brown.

Serve with a sprinkling of pink Himalayan salt.

INGREDIENTS

1½ cups grated edam cheese
½ cup grated parmesan
6 medium courgettes
pink Himalayan salt

Crispy Polenta

SERVES 2

INGREDIENTS

2½ cups water

1 GF chicken stock cube

1 cup cornmeal

½ cup grated parmesan

½ cup GF bacon finely chopped and fried

light olive oil

Line a square cake tin with foil leaving enough hanging over the edge to fold over and cover the top of the polenta once it is poured into the tin.

Brush the foil with olive oil.

Combine stock and water in a medium pot and bring to the boil.

As soon as it's boiling add cornmeal quickly in a thin stream while stirring constantly.

Keep stirring until the mixture thickens and it comes away from the side of the pan, work quickly as the mixture will start to set.

Stir the parmesan into the mixture until smooth.

Stir bacon into the mixture.

Transfer mixture to prepared tin, smooth the surface with the back of a spoon or fold the foil over and press flat with your hands.

Refrigerate for 2 hours.

Peel foil off polenta and cut into four squares.

Fry the polenta in plenty of olive oil in an electric fry-pan on high heat until brown and crispy.

Serve on it's own as a snack or with chunky tomato soup, pumpkin soup, baked beans or something similar.

Silverbeet Wedges

MAKES 12 WEDGES

Preheat oven to 200°.

Line a round 8" cake tin with baking paper.

Remove the stalks and boil the silverbeet leaves until soft then drain the water and chop very finely (you could use the food processor to chop it).

Combine eggs, cornmeal, milk and salt, then add the parmesan and silverbeet.

Press into the cake tin right to the edges and smooth the top with the back of a metal spoon.

Bake for 30 minutes.

Leave to cool then slice into 12 pieces.

Serve warm with sweet chilli sauce.

INGREDIENTS

2 eggs
200g silverbeet
1 cup cornmeal
½ cup trim milk
¾ cup grated parmesan
½ teaspoon salt
GF sweet chilli sauce to serve

Rice Paper Rolls

MAKES 20 ROLLS

INGREDIENTS

1 grated carrot

1 cup corn

shredded lettuce or cabbage

100g finely diced pork, chicken or beef

1 GF beef or chicken stock cube

3 cups boiling water

light olive oil

½ cup GF sweet chilli sauce

1 tablespoon GF soy sauce

rice paper sheets (*large square ones are the easiest to use*)

50g GF rice vermicelli noodles

Fry the meat in olive oil in an electric fry-pan until fully cooked then set aside.

Soak rice noodles with stock cube in boiling water until soft.

Mix softened rice noodles, shredded lettuce or cabbage, grated carrot, corn, meat, soy sauce and sweet chilli sauce in a bowl.

Dip two sheets of rice paper in hot water at a time and when they are soft place a small amount of the vegetable and meat mixture in the centre, roll the rice paper up and fold over the ends.

Using two sheets at a time to double the thickness helps to keep the filling in but you can use one sheet if you prefer.

Fry the rolls in plenty of olive oil in the electric fry-pan or brush the rolls with oil, line them up spaced out on an oven tray and bake until crispy.

The rolls are ready when the outsides are light brown and crispy.

They can also be eaten uncooked if you prefer.

Serve with sweet chilli sauce for dipping.

Summer Salmon

SERVING NUMBERS DEPENDANT ON QUANTITY OF
SALMON BOUGHT

For this recipe use what quantities suit you.

Make the dressing first and place in the fridge to chill.

Toast the bread and spread with plenty of cream cheese.

Layer the smoked salmon on the toast.

Sprinkle with black pepper and lemon juice.

Halve the cherry tomatoes and cut the avocado
into cubes.

Cut the cheese into cubes or grate it, add some lettuce
and toss.

Place some salad on each plate next to the salmon
on toast.

INGREDIENTS

thin slices GF toasted seed bread

cold thinly sliced smoked salmon

spreadable light cream cheese

fancy lettuce

cherry tomatoes

edam cheese

avocado

black pepper

lemon juice

DRESSING

1 tablespoon white vinegar

1 tablespoon lemon juice

¼ cup orange juice

¼ cup light olive oil

Saganaki

SERVES 2

INGREDIENTS

1 egg

rice flour to coat

1 tablespoon trim milk

180g kefalotyri or kasseri greek cheese

4 tablespoons lemon juice

extra light olive oil for frying

cherry tomatoes

fancy lettuce

sprouts

Slice cheese in half so it's in two thin flattish squares.

Mix the egg and milk on a plate.

Coat the cheese pieces in the egg and milk mixture.

Dip the cheese in the flour and coat thoroughly.

Fry in olive oil on medium heat for 1-2 minutes each side until golden brown.

Coat the cheese in lemon juice just before it leaves the pan.

Serve with fancy lettuce, cherry tomatoes and sprouts on the side.

Cajun Chicken Salad

SERVES 4

Arrange shredded lettuce, shredded silverbeet and grated carrot on dinner plates.

Put the diced chicken in a plastic re-sealable bag with the egg and mix it around.

Mix the maize cornflour and cajun mix together then add to the plastic bag and shake to coat the chicken.

Boil one cup of water with ½ cup of quinoa until all the water is absorbed.

While the quinoa is cooking, begin frying the chicken in an electric fry-pan with plenty of olive oil.

When the chicken is cooked through mix in the quinoa and dish onto the four separate plates on top of the lettuce and carrot.

Serve with plain unsweetened yoghurt.

INGREDIENTS

60g shredded fancy lettuce

20g shredded silverbeet

1 grated carrot

2 skinless finely diced chicken breasts

3 tablespoons GF cajun mix – medium hot

GF plain unsweetened yoghurt

½ cup quinoa

¾ cup maize cornflour

light olive oil

1 egg

Cranberry Chicken Salad

SERVES 4

INGREDIENTS

2 eggs
½ cup rice flour
GF breadcrumbs
2 finely diced chicken breasts
shredded fancy lettuce
handful of halved cherry tomatoes
1 grated carrot
120g diced camembert
GF cranberry sauce

Mix the lettuce, carrot, cherry tomatoes and camembert together in a large salad bowl.

You can use quantities that suit you.

Shake the chicken in a plastic bag with the rice flour to coat it.

Break the eggs into the plastic bag and mix them around to cover the chicken.

Pour the crumbs into the plastic bag and shake the bag then firmly press the crumbs into the chicken.

Tip the chicken into an electric fry-pan with plenty of olive oil and fry until cooked right through (when adding the chicken to the salad, put the crumbs that fall off into the salad too).

When the chicken is cooked through, toss through the salad.

Serve with plenty of cranberry sauce.

Smoked Chicken Salad

SERVES 4

Dice the smoked chicken into small cubes.

Mix pineapple, chicken, lettuce, cheese, carrot, alfalfa sprouts, snowpea shoots, orange and avocado together in a large salad bowl.

INGREDIENTS

300g manuka smoked chicken
40g alfalfa sprouts and snowpea shoots
100g shredded fancy lettuce
1 grated carrot
1 cup grated edam cheese
200g tinned pineapple pieces
1 cubed orange
1 cubed avocado

Mango and Bacon Salad

SERVES 2

INGREDIENTS

50g spinach

50g fancy lettuce

80g cherry tomatoes

425g can diced mango

150g chopped fried GF bacon

80g grated edam cheese

40g pinenuts

GF croutons (*if you can't find them to buy, you can make your own with Seed Bread*)

Finely chop bacon and fry till crispy then set aside.

Wash and finely chop spinach and lettuce and place in a salad bowl.

Add pinenuts, cheese and cherry tomatoes cut in halves.

Add the bacon and diced mango to salad and toss.

Serve with croutons and pink Himalayan salt.

Kids Platter

SERVES 2

Using mini jelly moulds make different flavoured jellies each week and have them set aside for afternoon snacks.

Arrange marshmallows cut in half and apple and orange cubes on kebab sticks.

Choose a favourite novelty plate and arrange the fruit kebabs, cheese cubes, rice cakes or rice crackers, and pots of jelly on it.

Mix the bananas and milk together in a blender to make a smoothie then add fun straws.

INGREDIENTS

1 apple

1 orange

GF cheese cubes

6 GF marshmallows

2 snack bags of GF mini rice cakes or
    8 GF rice crackers (*check all flavours*)

1 packet of GF jelly crystals

2 bananas

1½ cups milk

Pancakes

MAKES 8-10 PANCAKES

INGREDIENTS

½ cup rice flour

1½ cup maize cornflour

2 teaspoons GF baking powder

½ teaspoon salt

½ cup white sugar

1½ cups trim milk

2 eggs

butter to grease

Sift maize cornflour, rice flour, baking powder and salt together.

Beat eggs and sugar until frothy.

Pour eggs and milk into the dry ingredients and mix until no lumps remain.

Heat a medium sized fry-pan to a low heat and grease with butter.

Pour enough mixture into the pan to thinly coat the bottom and tilt the pan to make sure the mixture coats it evenly right to the edges.

Wait for the mixture to stop being runny and for small holes to appear on the surface then flip over with a non stick turner, it should be very lightly brown and will only need a short time to cook.

Grease the pan lightly for each pancake.

SERVING SUGGESTIONS

GF maple syrup and GF bacon.

GF maple syrup and vanilla ice cream.

Strawberries and whipped cream.

Lemon juice and sugar.

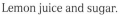

Main Meals

Lamb Stuffed Eggplants

SERVES 2

INGREDIENTS

2 eggplants
light olive oil
400g lamb mince
400g can GF mixed beans
400g can diced tomatoes in juice
3 crushed garlic cloves
½ teaspoon dried oregano
1 teaspoon dried mixed herbs
1 bundle shredded spinach
100g crumbly feta cheese
GF plain unsweetened yoghurt to serve

Preheat the oven to 180°.

Cut each eggplant in half lengthways then scoop out the flesh and discard.

Lay the halves hollow side up on a greased oven tray.

Bake the eggplants for 15 minutes before starting the lamb mince.

Keep an eye on the eggplants while you cook the mince, turn off the oven if they start to look crispy, otherwise leave them until the mince is cooked.

Fry the crushed garlic in olive oil in an electric fry-pan then add lamb mince.

Drain and rinse the mixed beans.

When the mince is browned add beans, tomatoes, spinach and herbs.

Serve when the mince is cooked and the spinach is soft.

Spoon the lamb into the eggplants and serve with feta cheese sprinkled on the top and plain unsweetened yoghurt on the side.

Mediterranean Millet

SERVES 2

In a pot put millet and boiling water, add the lid and simmer until all the water has evaporated, you need to check it regularly. It can take anywhere between 10 and 30 minutes to be ready.

While the millet is cooking chop sundried tomatoes finely.

Fry garlic in an electric fry-pan then add lamb and brown.

Add sundried tomatoes, olives, spinach and canned tomatoes to simmer in the fry pan until the millet is ready.

Serve with crumbly feta and plain unsweetened yoghurt.

INGREDIENTS

1 cup hulled millet

2½ cups boiling water

2 tablespoons sliced black olives

2 tablespoons sun-dried tomatoes

5-10 leaves of shredded spinach

1 teaspoon crushed garlic

400g diced lamb

400g can diced tomatoes in juice

100g chopped crumbly feta

GF plain unsweetened yoghurt to serve

Plum Chicken Millet

SERVES 2

INGREDIENTS

2 heaped tablespoons honey

2 tablespoons GF soy sauce

¼ cup GF plum sauce

1 large diced skinless chicken breast

1 grated courgette

1 grated carrot

100g finely chopped broccoli

1 cup hulled millet

2½ cups boiling water

Mix the honey, soy sauce and plum sauce and marinade the diced chicken in it.

In a pot put millet and boiling water, add the lid and simmer until all the water has evaporated, you need to check it regularly. It can take anywhere between 10 and 30 minutes to be ready.

While the millet is cooking fry the chicken and all remaining marinade in an electric fry-pan in olive oil.

When the chicken is almost cooked add the carrot, courgette and broccoli.

Once the vegetables are mixed in, place the lid on the electric fry-pan but stir it regularly.

If the millet is ready early it will stay warm if you leave it in the pot with the lid on.

When the vegetables are cooked to your liking serve on top of the millet.

Serve with extra plum sauce.

Pumpkin Quinoa

SERVES 2

Boil diced pumpkin until soft.

While pumpkin is cooking bring quinoa and 1 cup of water to the boil then simmer until all the water is absorbed.

While both the pumpkin and quinoa are cooking fry the onion with olive oil in an electric fry-pan.

Add chicken to the fry-pan and brown, then add courgette, tomatoes and garlic salt.

Add the quinoa to the fry-pan when all the water has absorbed.

Simmer the tomato mixture until the pumpkin is ready then add the pumpkin to the fry-pan and stir through, continue to cook for another 5 minutes.

Serve with plain unsweetened yoghurt.

INGREDIENTS

½ cup quinoa

1 cup water

1 finely chopped onion

1 can GF italian tomatoes

1 diced skinless chicken breast

1 sliced courgette

½ small pumpkin diced

1 teaspoon garlic salt

GF plain unsweetened yoghurt to serve

Pumpkin Cottage Pie

SERVES 6

INGREDIENTS

420g can GF hot chilli beans

400g can diced tomatoes in juice

½ medium pumpkin

1 carrot chopped finely

½ cup of frozen corn

6 medium potatoes

2 heaped teaspoons dried onion flakes

1 GF chicken stock cube

½ cup boiling water

1 cup grated edam cheese

½ cup grated parmesan cheese

¾ cup trim milk

2 tablespoons light olive oil

2 heaped teaspoons garlic salt

sour cream or GF plain unsweetened
     yoghurt to serve

Preheat oven to 210°.

Peel and chop potatoes and carrots then place in separate pots to boil until soft.

Peel and chop pumpkin into 3cm cubes then place pumpkin in a pot to boil.

Mix beans, tomatoes, onion flakes, corn and garlic salt in a large bowl.

Drain carrot and add to mixture.

Drain pumpkin and add to mixture.

Dissolve chicken stock cube in boiling water and add to mixture.

Pour mixture into a large glass rectangular dish or something similar.

Mash potatoes with olive oil and trim milk and spread over top of mixture.

Bake in oven for 30 minutes.

Sprinkle cheese over the top and bake for a further 10 minutes before serving.

Serve with sour cream or plain unsweetened yoghurt.

Chicken Cottage Pie

SERVES 6

Preheat oven to 210°.

Peel and chop potatoes and carrots then place in separate pots to boil until soft.

Fry onion until clear then add diced chicken and brown.

Mix beans, tomatoes, corn, peas, carrots, onion, chicken and garlic salt in a large glass rectangular dish or something similar.

Dissolve chicken stock cube in boiling water and stir into mixture.

Mash potatoes with olive oil and trim milk and spread over top of mixture.

Bake in oven for 30 minutes.

Sprinkle cheese over the top and bake for a further 10-15 minutes before serving.

INGREDIENTS

420g can GF hot chilli beans

400g can GF mexican style tomatoes

2 skinless chicken breasts diced finely

2 carrots chopped finely

1 onion chopped finely

¾ cup frozen corn

½ cup frozen peas

five large potatoes

½ cup trim milk

1 teaspoon garlic salt

2 tablespoons light olive oil

1 GF chicken stock cube

½ cup boiling water

1 cup grated edam cheese

½ cup grated parmesan cheesee

Chilli Bake

SERVES 6

INGREDIENTS

420g can GF hot chilli beans
400g can GF mexican style tomatoes
1 finely chopped onion
400g beef mince
2 tablespoons light olive oil

TOPPING

1 egg
50g melted butter
¼ cup trim milk
½ cup GF plain unsweetened yoghurt
1 cup grated edam cheese
1 finely chopped onion
410g can GF cream style corn
1 teaspoon GF baking powder
1 teaspoon salt
1 cup cornmeal

Preheat oven to 180°.

Fry the onion in olive oil in an electric fry-pan then add the mince.

When the mince is browned add the tomatoes and chilli beans then turn to a low heat and begin making the topping.

Put butter and onion in a glass mixing bowl and microwave until melted.

Mix cream style corn, egg, milk, yoghurt and cheese with the onion and butter.

Pour cornmeal on top of the mixture then before mixing it in, add the salt and baking powder to it then thoroughly mix it.

Pour mince and bean mixture into a large shallow glass rectangular dish.

Spoon the topping over the mince and use the back of a metal spoon to spread it out.

Bake for 35 to 45 minutes.

Serve with plain unsweetened yoghurt.

Vegetable Scone Bake

SERVES 6

Preheat oven to 200°.

Peel and finely chop eggplants, kumara, carrots, onion, courgette, broccoli and garlic.

Fry the vegetables in an electric fry-pan for 30 minutes with thyme, oregano, salt, pepper and plenty of olive oil.

Transfer vegetable mix to a large shallow glass rectangular dish.

Dissolve the vegetable stock cube in boiling water and pour over the vegetables.

Cover the top with tin foil and bake in the oven for 40 minutes.

While the vegetables are in the oven make the topping.

Sift the rice flour, soy flour, cornflour, potato flour and baking powder twice.

Rub in the butter with your fingertips until the mixture resembles breadcrumbs.

Stir in grated cheese, breadcrumbs, parsley and oregano.

Mix the egg and milk together then stir into the flour so it resembles crumbs.

If the mixture is too doughy you may need to add more flour to break it up.

Remove the vegetables from the oven and turn the temperature up to 230°.

Remove the tin foil and sprinkle the crumbly topping mixture over the vegetables.

Put back in the oven for 10 minutes until the topping is browned.

Let the dish sit for 10 minutes before you serve it.

INGREDIENTS

2 eggplants
2 kumara
2 carrots
1 onion
1 courgette
½ head of broccoli
2 garlic cloves
1 teaspoon dried thyme
1 teaspoon dried oregano
½ teaspoon black pepper
½ teaspoon salt
1 GF vegetable stock cube
1 cup boiling water
light olive oil for frying

TOPPING

¾ cup rice flour
½ cup soy flour
½ cup maize cornflour
¼ cup potato flour
2 teaspoons GF baking powder
2 tablespoons GF breadcrumbs
1 cup grated edam cheese
¼ cup fresh chopped parsley
1 teaspoon dried oregano
⅓ cup trim milk
80g butter
1 egg

Lamb and Kumara Pie

SERVES 6

INGREDIENTS

½ cup rice flour

½ cup potato flour

½ cup maize cornflour

¼ cup soy flour

130g chilled chopped butter

1 tablespoon guar gum

2 teaspoons salt

1 egg yolk

½ cup water

350g lamb mince

1 kumara

1 bunch of spinach

150g crumbly feta

1 cup GF gravy

2 tablespoons maize cornflour to thicken the gravy

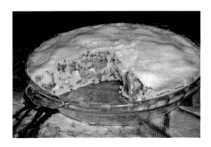

Lightly grease a glass, metal or ceramic pie dish with butter.

Sift rice flour, potato flour, maize cornflour, soy flour, 1 teaspoon of salt and guar gum into a bowl. Using your fingertips rub the butter into the mix until it resembles breadcrumbs.

Use a flat bladed knife to mix in the yolk and up to ½ cup of water to make the dough (you may not need all the water).

Roll the soft dough into a ball, wrap in plastic and place in the fridge for 30 minutes, it might be crumbly and hard to roll up, you may have to put the remaining crumbs onto the plastic and then wrap up and roll the covered ball in your hands.

While the dough is in the fridge, start making the pie filling.

Peel and finely dice the kumara and boil until soft.

In the electric fry-pan cook the lamb mince with a little olive oil and the remaining teaspoon of salt, shred the spinach up finely in a food processor or with a knife and add to the browned mince, then when the kumara is soft, add that to the mince too.

Preheat the oven to 190°.

Make up the gravy by combining the gravy powder and maize cornflour with a small amount of cold water to make a paste, then gradually adding boiling water stirring until smooth.

Add the gravy to the fry-pan and stir through then leave to simmer on a low heat while you roll out the dough. Remove the dough from the fridge and flour the bench with rice flour, warm the dough in your hands and knead it a little (If it was crumbly when it went into the fridge, then warm it with your hands and it will gradually start to combine).

When the dough has combined properly start rolling it out on the liberally floured bench and lay the bottom piece of pastry into the pie dish, press it down and trim the edges.

Crumble the feta through the lamb mince then fill the pie with the filling and roll out the top piece of pastry. Lay the top piece of pastry over the filling and trim the edges, use the off cuts to create decorations for the top if you like and brush the top of the pie with milk before placing in the oven.

Bake for 30 minutes.

Mince and Cheese Pie

SERVES 6

Lightly grease a glass, metal or ceramic pie dish with butter.

Sift rice flour, potato flour, maize cornflour, soy flour, salt and guar gum into a bowl. Using your fingertips rub the butter into the mix until it resembles breadcrumbs.

Use a flat bladed knife to mix in the yolk and up to ½ cup of water to make the dough (you may not need all the water). Roll the soft dough into a ball, wrap in plastic and place in the fridge for 30 minutes, it might be crumbly and hard to roll up, you may have to put the remaining crumbs onto the plastic and then wrap up and roll the covered ball in your hands.

While the dough is in the fridge, start making the pie filling. In the electric fry-pan brown the beef mince.

Preheat the oven to 190°.

Make up the gravy by combining the gravy powder and maize cornflour with a small amount of cold water to make a paste, then gradually adding boiling water stirring until smooth.

Add the gravy to the fry-pan and stir through then leave to simmer on a low heat while you roll out the dough.

Remove the dough from the fridge and flour the bench with rice flour, warm the dough in your hands and knead it a little (If it was crumbly when it went into the fridge, then warm it with your hands and it will gradually start to combine).

When the dough has combined properly start rolling it out on the liberally floured bench and lay the bottom piece of pastry into the pie dish, press it down and trim the edges.

Pour the mince and gravy into the pie case then cover it with slices of cheese.

Roll out the top piece of pastry and lay it over the filling and trim the edges, use the off cuts to create decorations for the top if you like and brush the top of the pie with milk before placing in the oven.

Bake for 30 minutes.

INGREDIENTS

½ cup rice flour

½ cup potato flour

½ cup maize cornflour

¼ cup soy flour

130g chilled chopped butter

1 tablespoon guar gum

1 teaspoon salt

1 egg yolk

½ cup water

500g beef mince

edam cheese

2 cups GF gravy

2 tablespoons maize cornflour to thicken the gravy

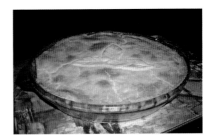

Chicken, Cranberry and Brie Pizza

MAKES 1 LARGE PIZZA

INGREDIENTS

150g GF cranberry sauce

¾ cup finely chopped fried GF bacon

1 finely diced cooked chicken breast

150g thinly sliced brie cheese

1½ cups grated edam cheese

4 tablespoons GF tomato paste

GF bread mix (*any brand*)

Preheat oven to 120° and line an oven tray with baking paper.

Using your preferred brand of bread mix, prepare the mixture and spoon onto the baking paper spreading it to a 5mm thickness.

Bake at 120° for 15-20 minutes then remove and cover with toppings.

Spread the tomato paste evenly over the base, then the edam cheese, bacon, chicken, cranberry sauce and brie in that order.

Put pizza back in oven to cook for 15 minutes at 180°.

Chicken, Bacon and Olive Pizza

MAKES 1 LARGE PIZZA

Preheat oven to 120° and line an oven tray with baking paper.

Using your preferred brand of bread mix, prepare the mixture and spoon onto the baking paper spreading it to a 5mm thickness.

Bake at 120° for 15-20 minutes then remove and cover with toppings.

Spread the tomato paste evenly over the base, then the edam cheese, chopped tomatoes, bacon, chicken, basil, parmesan and salami in that order.

Put pizza back in oven to cook for 15 minutes at 180°.

INGREDIENTS

handful of fresh basil leaves
16 GF salami slices
¾ cup finely chopped fried GF bacon
1 finely diced cooked chicken breast
400g can drained chopped tomatoes
½ cup chopped sliced black olives
½ cup grated parmesan
1½ cups grated edam cheese
4 tablespoons GF tomato paste
GF bread mix (*any brand*)

39

BBQ Bacon Cheeseburgers

MAKES 4 BURGERS

INGREDIENTS

1 egg

1 onion

1 teaspoon salt

½ teaspoon black pepper

2 tablespoons trim milk

2 teaspoons sesame seeds

2 tablespoons maize cornflour

4 slices GF processed tasty cheese

GF barbeque sauce

4 strips GF bacon

300g beef mince

GF bread mix (*any brand*)

Preheat oven to 120° and line an oven tray with baking paper.

Using your preferred brand of bread mix, prepare the mixture and spoon onto the baking paper in 8 small circles (you may need to do four at a time depending on size).

Bake at 120° for 20 minutes then remove and increase temperature to 160°.

Brush the tops of the buns with milk and sprinkle sesame seeds on four of them. Return to the oven for 10 minutes then fan bake for a further 3-4 minutes to brown.

Chop the onion very finely in a food processor and fry lightly then mix the mince, onion, maize cornflour, black pepper and salt together.

Cut the bacon strips in half so you end up with eight short strips and fry them until crispy.

Spoon the patty mixture onto the fry-pan and use the back of a spoon to spread them into flat round shapes to fit the buns you've made.

Place each patty on the raised side of a burger bun bottom so it sits flat.

Place a square of cheese, 2 short strips of bacon and barbeque sauce on the meat patties then top with the remaining 4 burger bun sesame halves.

Serve the burgers on their own, with a salad, or with homemade chips.

Nachos

SERVES 4

Preheat oven to 150°.

Fry the mince in olive oil in electric fry-pan.

When the mince is browned add chilli beans and tomatoes and simmer until the mince is cooked through.

Arrange corn chips on four dinner plates or a large platter.

Pour mince and bean mixture over the corn chips.

Sprinkle cheese and a pinch of chilli powder over the nachos and put in the oven to grill.

When the cheese has melted remove from oven and serve with avocado and sour cream on top.

INGREDIENTS

light olive oil
500g beef mince
420g can GF hot chilli beans
400g can GF mexican style tomatoes
1 diced avocado
2 cups grated edam cheese
250g light sour cream
GF corn chips
sprinkle of GF chilli powder

Stuffed Potatoes

MAKES 4

INGREDIENTS

410g can GF cream style corn
420g can GF baked beans
½ cup finely chopped GF bacon
4 large potatoes
1 cup grated edam cheese
½ cup grated parmesan
salt and pepper
light olive oil
sour cream to serve

Bake potatoes whole at 220°.

When skin is crispy and potato is cooked scoop potato out of skins and set aside.

Mix edam cheese and parmesan and set half aside.

Fry bacon lightly in olive oil then mix with creamed corn, baked beans, a sprinkling of salt and pepper and half the cheese.

Fill the potato skins with the mixture.

Top the stuffed potatoes with discarded potato and the remainder of the cheese.

Return to the oven and bake for half an hour at 180°.

Serve with sour cream.

Aioli Vegetable Roast

SERVES 4

Preheat oven to 220°.

Peel and chop vegetables into chunks.

Peel garlic cloves, crush them slightly but leave whole for roasting.

Arrange vegetables and garlic cloves in a large roasting pan, pour over oil then mix through with a metal spatula.

Bake vegetables for 45-60 minutes until they are crispy turning twice during cooking.

Put egg yolks, garlic and lemon juice in a food processor and blend until smooth.

Whilst the processor is going, start pouring in the cup of oil as gradually and slowly as possible so the mixture does not curdle.

The aioli will thicken and look creamy.

When the vegetables are ready serve on a large platter.

Serve the aioli in dipping bowls.

INGREDIENTS

½ medium sized pumpkin
3 potatoes
2 carrots
3 kumara
2 courgettes
4 garlic cloves
light olive oil

AIOLI

2 egg yolks
1 teaspoon crushed garlic
1 tablespoon lemon juice
1 cup light olive oil
black pepper
salt

43

Tofu Satay

INGREDIENTS

300g GF firm tofu
6 kebab skewers

MARINADE

2 cloves garlic
1cm fresh root ginger
2 tablespoons GF soy sauce
2 tablespoons honey

SATAY SAUCE

150g unsalted roasted peanuts
2 tablespoons GF peanut butter
½ teaspoon GF chilli powder
200ml light coconut milk
juice of 1 lime

SERVES 2

Put all marinade ingredients in food processor and mix until smooth.

Dice tofu into 30 cubes and place marinade and tofu into a plastic bag.

Leave the plastic bag in the refrigerator for 30 minutes.

While tofu is in the fridge make satay sauce by combining all the sauce ingredients in the food processor and blend until smooth.

Heat the electric fry-pan and thread 5 squares of tofu onto each skewer.

Cook on high heat turning the skewers until they go crispy on all sides then pour the peanut sauce over the kebabs and simmer until the sauce is hot and has darkened, it will become thicker and you will need to stir it occasionally to prevent it from burning.

Spoon the sauce onto the dinner plates, lay the kebabs on top and serve with a mixed lettuce and carrot salad.

Rosemary and Parmesan Chicken

SERVES 2

Preheat the oven to 220°.

Mix the ingredients for the stuffing together in a small bowl.

Cut a pocket through the middle of each piece of chicken then place half of the stuffing in each chicken breast.

Roll the chicken breasts in rice flour then in egg and breadcrumbs.

Bake the chicken breasts for 40 minutes or until cooked right through.

Serve with vegetables or salad.

INGREDIENTS

1 egg
rice flour to coat
2 small skinless chicken breasts
GF breadcrumbs

STUFFING

1 teaspoon garlic salt
1 teaspoon dried onion flakes
1 teaspoon dried mixed herbs
1 teaspoon dried rosemary
2 tablespoons of pinenuts
2 tablespoons grated parmesan
3 tablespoons GF breadcrumbs
½ cup warm water

Steak and Kumara Mash

SERVES 2

INGREDIENTS

2 pieces of fillet steak

3 tablespoons GF sweet chilli sauce

1 tablespoon GF tomato sauce

¼ cup GF soy sauce

pinch of black pepper

pinch of salt

2 large kumara

2 tablespoons light olive oil

2 tablespoons trim milk

Marinade steak in sweet chilli sauce, tomato sauce, soy sauce and salt and black pepper for as long as you like.

Chop and peel kumara then boil for half an hour or until soft.

10 minutes before the kumara will be ready start heating the fry-pan for the steak.

Cook steak on high heat turning only once.

Pour remainder of marinade over steak whilst it is cooking to add flavour.

Whilst steak is cooking drain and mash the kumara.

Add olive oil after mashing and mix well, then add trim milk and mash again.

Serve steak and kumara with corn, peas, carrots or any other vegetables desired.

Devilled Sausages

SERVES 4

Preheat oven to 180°.

Slice sausages into 1 cm thick pieces.

Sift brown sugar, mustard powder, garlic salt and maize cornflour together several times.

Mix tomato paste, white vinegar, soy sauce and worcester sauce together then pour into dry ingredients and blend.

Pour sauce into casserole dish then add apple, hot water and sausages and mix well.

Cook in oven for 1½ hours stirring twice.

Serve with mashed potato.

INGREDIENTS

10 GF pre-cooked sausages

550g can apple pie filling

¼ cup soft brown sugar

¼ cup maize cornflour

1 tablespoon white vinegar

1 tablespoon GF soy sauce

1 tablespoon GF worcester sauce

3 tablespoons GF tomato paste

1 teaspoon garlic salt

1 teaspoon GF mustard powder

2 cups hot water

Mushroom, Chicken Casserole

SERVES 2

INGREDIENTS

2 diced skinless chicken breasts

2 cups trim milk

2 tablespoons butter

2 tablespoons rice flour

2 portobello mushrooms

10 button mushrooms

1 packet of GF creamy chicken soup
  (*made up as per instructions on packet*)

1 teaspoon black pepper

1 teaspoon salt

Preheat oven to 180°.

Put the portobello mushrooms in a food processor and chop them as fine as crumbs.

Thinly slice the button mushrooms and set aside.

Melt butter in a pot, add rice flour and cook for 1 minute, stirring until golden.

Add trim milk to the pot gradually, stirring until smooth each time more is added.

Simmer for 2 minutes but do not allow to boil.

Remove the pot from the heat and stir in the portobello and button mushrooms then transfer to a casserole dish.

Brown the chicken briefly in a fry-pan then add to the casserole dish.

Pour in the creamy chicken soup and give it all a stir.

Bake in oven for 30 minutes.

Serve with hulled millet or rice.

Beef Stew

SERVES 2

Preheat oven to 180°.

Peel and chop potatoes, carrot, onion, broccoli and beef into even sized cubes.

Put the meat and vegetables into a casserole dish and add black pepper and salt.

In a jug mix boiling water, beef stock, soy sauce, worcester sauce, tomato sauce and maize cornflour, then add to the casserole dish and put the lid on.

Cook in the oven for 1½ hours stirring three times.

INGREDIENTS

1 carrot

¼ head of broccoli

2 large potatoes

500g beef suitable for stews/casseroles

1 onion chopped finely

1 GF beef stock cube

1 tablespoon GF soy sauce

1 tablespoon GF worcester sauce

1 tablespoon GF tomato sauce

3 tablespoons maize cornflour

2 cups boiling water

black pepper

salt

Beef Vermicelli

SERVES 2

INGREDIENTS

125g GF rice vermicelli noodles
500g diced beef
1 carrot chopped thinly lengthways
½ head of broccoli
1 can baby corn
2 tablespoons GF soy sauce
2 tablespoons GF sweet chilli sauce
1 heaped tablespoon maize cornflour
1 onion chopped finely
2 garlic cloves crushed
1 GF beef stock cube
2 tablespoons light olive oil
1½ cups boiling water

Boil carrot and broccoli to soften.

Soak noodles for 4 minutes in hot water then drain.

Rinse noodles in cold water and drain again.

Fry onion and garlic in oil in the electric fry-pan.

Add beef and brown it.

Add baby corn, carrot and broccoli to fry-pan.

Dissolve beef stock cube in boiling water.

Mix cornflour, soy sauce, sweet chilli sauce and ¼ cup of the beef stock into a paste.

Gradually add the remaining stock to the paste stirring it until combined.

Add noodles and beef stock to fry-pan and stir through.

Put the lid on the fry-pan and continue to cook until vegetables are cooked and the liquid has been mostly absorbed.

Serve with extra sweet chilli sauce.

Lemon Chicken

SERVES 2

Place diced chicken in a plastic zip-lock bag and add the egg to coat chicken.

Boil the carrots and frozen corn before putting the chicken on to cook.

Then add maize cornflour to the bag and shake well so chicken is thoroughly coated.

Heat olive oil in fry-pan and add chicken to cook until browned.

Make the sauce with tapioca flour, brown sugar, lemon juice and hot water.

Pour into fry-pan, add carrots and corn then leave to simmer until chicken is cooked and some of the sauce has been absorbed.

Serve with basmati rice, sea salt and extra lemon juice or wedges of lemon.

INGREDIENTS

1 egg
1 diced skinless chicken breast
2 tablespoons light olive oil
1 carrot chopped finely
1 cup frozen corn
¾ cup maize cornflour
1 tablespoon tapioca flour
1 tablespoon soft brown sugar
1½ cups hot water
¼ cup lemon juice
sea salt

Salmon Mornay

SERVES 2

INGREDIENTS

1½ cups GF breadcrumbs

4 potatoes

210g tin red salmon

1¼ cups trim milk

2 tablespoons olive oil

25g butter

2 tablespoons rice flour

½ teaspoon black pepper

½ teaspoon salt

Preheat oven to 180°.

Drain and mash the salmon and set aside.

Peel potatoes and boil till soft.

While the potatoes are boiling melt butter in a pot, add rice flour and cook for one minute, stirring until golden.

Add one cup of milk to the pot gradually, stirring until smooth each time more is added.

Add pepper and salt then simmer for two minutes but do not allow it to boil.

Remove the pot from the heat and stir in the salmon, then return to the element on a low heat for two minutes.

Mash the potatoes with the remaining trim milk and olive oil then transfer to a round 8" ceramic or glass dish.

Smooth the potato with the back of a spoon and pour the salmon sauce over the top.

Cover the salmon with breadcrumbs.

Bake for 30 minutes.

Pasta

   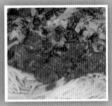

Macaroni Cheese

SERVES 6

INGREDIENTS

60g butter
2 tablespoons rice flour
2 cups trim milk
2 cups grated edam cheese
¾ cup grated parmesan
375ml can light and creamy evaporated milk
2 cups GF breadcrumbs
250g GF dried macaroni pasta
¾ cup chopped GF bacon

Preheat oven to 180°.

Cook pasta in a pot for 9 minutes, drain and set aside.

While pasta is cooking finely chop and fry bacon and set aside.

Melt butter in a pot, add rice flour and cook for 1 minute, stirring until golden.

Combine trim milk and evaporated milk and add to the pot gradually, stirring until smooth each time more is added.

Simmer for 2 minutes but do not allow it to boil.

Remove from the heat and add ¾ of the edam cheese and ¾ of the parmesan cheese.

Stir until it's melted and smooth then add the cooked pasta and bacon.

Pour mixture into a large shallow glass rectangular dish or something similar.

Chop the remaining edam and parmesan cheese finely and combine with the breadcrumbs then sprinkle evenly over the top of the pasta.

Bake for 20 to 30 minutes.

James' Pasta Bake

SERVES 4

Preheat oven to 180°.

Finely chop bacon and fry then set aside.

Boil pasta for the recommended time on the packet.

Whilst pasta is boiling melt butter in a small saucepan.

Add flour and stir constantly for two minutes.

Remove from heat and add milk slowly whilst
continuing stirring.

Return saucepan to heat and continue stirring until
sauce thickens.

Remove from heat and add grated cheese.

Add a sprinkle of salt and pepper.

Mix bacon with pasta and place in a rectangular
glass dish.

Pour over the pasta sauce then the cheese sauce.

Bake in oven for 20 minutes.

INGREDIENTS

250g GF dried penne pasta

600g – 700g GF romano and garlic pasta
sauce or something similar

100g finely chopped GF bacon

2 tablespoons rice flour

2 tablespoons butter

1 cup trim milk

1 cup grated edam cheese

salt and black pepper

Spaghetti Bolognese

SERVES 4

INGREDIENTS

1 onion
500g mince
light olive oil
sprinkle of oregano
3 crushed garlic cloves
400g can GF Italian tomatoes
700g GF garlic and onion pasta sauce
375g GF dried spaghetti pasta
grated parmesan to serve

Chop onion finely and crush garlic then fry in olive oil in electric fry-pan.

Add mince to fry-pan and brown.

When mince is browned add pasta sauce, Italian tomatoes and oregano.

Simmer sauce until some of the liquid is reduced and it's thicker.

Cook pasta for the recommended time on the packet whilst sauce is simmering.

Serve with grated parmesan.

Smoked Chicken Penne

SERVES 4

Remove and shred the smoked chicken from the bones and set aside.

Heat an electric fry-pan to a medium heat.

Meanwhile cook pasta for the recommended time on the packet then drain and set aside.

Fry the crushed garlic and oil in the fry-pan then add the evaporated milk and cheese.

Mix until the cheese has melted and it's smooth then add the pasta, spinach, chicken and pinenuts.

Cook until heated right through and thickened.

Serve with parmesan.

INGREDIENTS

handful of pinenuts

shredded spinach

1 cup grated edam cheese

3 crushed garlic cloves

2 tablespoons light olive oil

375ml can light and creamy
  evaporated milk

250g GF dried penne pasta

1.1kg manuka smoked whole chicken

grated parmesan to serve

Creamy Fettuccine

SERVES 4

INGREDIENTS

¼ cup tapioca flour

¼ cup rice flour

⅓ cup soy flour

⅓ cup maize cornflour

1 tablespoon potato flour

1 tablespoon xanthan gum

1 tablespoon light olive oil

3 eggs at room temperature

1 grated carrot

2 skinless diced chicken breasts

375ml can light and creamy evaporated milk

½ cup of cream

½ teaspoon black pepper

½ teaspoon salt

½ cup grated mozzarella

½ cup grated parmesan to serve

Note: For this recipe you need a pasta machine

Sift all the dry ingredients three times to ensure they are thoroughly mixed.

Beat eggs and oil until frothy and foamy.

Fold egg mixture into dry ingredients.

Scoop the sticky pasta mixture into a ball and roll it in rice flour on the bench, knead it a bit to make sure it's fully blended.

Roll into a cylindrical shape and cut slices off to feed through the pasta machine.

You will need plenty of extra rice flour to reduce stickiness when rolling out.

Roll out all the dough with the pasta machine then cut the pasta sheets into fettuccine with the attachment on your pasta machine.

Put a pasta pot of water on to boil.

Heat the electric fry pan, add olive oil and fry the chicken, then add the cream, evaporated milk, mozzarella, grated carrot, salt and black pepper.

Simmer for 20-30 minutes stirring frequently until the sauce has half evaporated and is a bit thicker.

Place fettuccine in boiling water and simmer for 6-7 minutes.

Drain the pasta and combine with the sauce in a large bowl.

Serve with grated parmesan.

Ham Cannelloni

SERVES 4

Sift all the dry ingredients three times to ensure they are thoroughly mixed.

Beat eggs and oil until frothy and foamy.

Fold egg mixture into dry ingredients.

Scoop the sticky pasta mixture into a ball and roll it in rice flour on the bench, knead it a bit to make sure it's fully blended.

Roll into a cylindrical shape and cut slices off to feed through the pasta machine.

You will need plenty of extra rice flour to reduce stickiness when rolling out.

Roll out the dough as thin as you can with the pasta machine then lay the sheets flat on the bench.

Cut the pasta sheets into sections to make each cannelloni roll, they need to be just wide enough to make a roll and overlap at the back.

Evenly spread out the ham and mozzarella on the squares of pasta then roll each one up and place in a large shallow glass dish.

Heat the trim milk and evaporated milk and pour over the pasta.

Sprinkle the parmesan cheese and chopped tomatoes over the cannelloni and place in the oven at 180° for 20-25 minutes.

INGREDIENTS

200g shaved GF ham

½ cup grated parmesan

1 cup grated mozzarella

1 cup trim milk

375ml can light and creamy
    evaporated milk

1 can drained chopped tomatoes

¼ cup tapioca flour

¼ cup rice flour

⅓ cup soy flour

⅓ cup maize cornflour

1 tablespoon potato flour

1 tablespoon xanthan gum

1 tablespoon light olive oil

3 eggs at room temperature

*Note: For this recipe you need a
    pasta machine*

Chicken and Bacon Ravioli

INGREDIENTS

cooked chicken chopped finely
fried GF bacon chopped finely
½ cup grated parmesan
¼ cup tapioca flour
¼ cup rice flour
⅓ cup soy flour
⅓ cup maize cornflour
1 tablespoon potato flour
1 tablespoon xanthan gum
1 tablespoon light olive oil
3 eggs at room temperature
sea salt
homemade or store bought GF pasta sauce

*Note: For this recipe you need a
  pasta machine*

SERVES 2

Use a food processor to puree cooked chicken and bacon with grated parmesan then put aside, you only need a small amount of chicken and bacon but the quantity does depend on how thinly you roll the pasta and how many ravioli you can make from it.

Sift all the dry ingredients twice to ensure they are thoroughly mixed.

Beat eggs and oil until frothy and foamy.

Fold egg mixture into dry ingredients.

Use a food processor with a dough blade to knead pasta dough but you should also knead it a bit yourself to check it's fully blended.

Roll into a ball and cut slices off to feed through the pasta machine.

You may need extra rice flour to reduce stickiness when rolling out.

Roll out all the dough with the pasta machine then lay flat on the bench.

Cut the pasta sheets into small rectangles and place some chicken, bacon and parmesan filling on each one.

Fold over each rectangle to create a square shape and use your fingertips to squash the edges together.

Use a pasta bike tool to cut the edges off the ravioli in squares.

Leave ravioli out to dry a little before cooking.

Place in boiling water then simmer for 6-7 minutes.

Serve with a store bought tomato sauce, creamy sauce, or any other kind of pasta sauce and grated parmesan and sea salt.

Spinach and 3 Cheese Agnolotti

SERVES 2

Boil spinach until soft.

Use a food processor to puree spinach with grated parmesan, mozzarella and edam cheese then set aside.

Sift all the dry ingredients twice to ensure they are thoroughly mixed.

Beat eggs and oil until frothy and foamy.

Fold egg mixture into dry ingredients.

Use a food processor with a dough blade to knead pasta dough but you should also knead it a bit yourself to check it's fully blended.

Roll into a ball and cut slices off to feed through the pasta machine.

You may need extra rice flour to reduce stickiness when rolling out.

Roll out all the dough with the pasta machine then lay flat on the bench.

Cut the pasta sheets into squares and place some spinach and cheese filling on each square.

Fold over each square to create a triangle shape and use your fingertips to squash the edges together.

Use a pasta bike tool to cut the edges off the agnolotti in semi-circles.

Leave agnolotti out to dry a little before cooking.

Place in boiling water then simmer for 6-7 minutes.

Serve with a home made or store bought alfredo sauce, cabonara sauce, or any other kind of pasta sauce and grated parmesan and sea salt.

INGREDIENTS

1 bundle of spinach
¼ cup grated parmesan
½ cup grated mozzarella
¼ cup grated edam cheese
¼ cup tapioca flour
¼ cup rice flour
⅓ cup soy flour
⅓ cup maize cornflour
1 tablespoon potato flour
1 tablespoon xanthan gum
1 tablespoon light olive oil
3 eggs at room temperature
sea salt
homemade or store bought GF pasta sauce
　　(I recommend alfredo or cabonara)

Note: For this recipe you need a
　　pasta machine

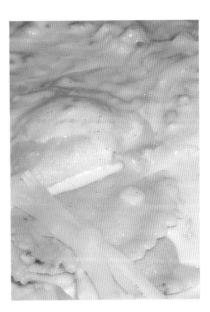

Homemade Pesto

SERVES 2

INGREDIENTS

60-80g fresh basil leaves
60g grated parmesan cheese
60g pinenuts
80-90mls extra light olive oil
1 heaped tablespoon crushed garlic

Put all ingredients into food processor and mix well.

This will make a creamy pesto sauce that you can use straight away or keep in the fridge for two to three days or freeze for later use.

SERVING SUGGESTION

Toss through penne and sprinkle with parmesan.

Baking

Spicy Fruit Bread

MAKES 1 LOAF

INGREDIENTS

2 cups rice flour
½ cup maize cornflour
½ cup tapioca flour
½ cup soy flour
½ cup trim milk powder
2 teaspoons cinnamon
4 teaspoons mixed spice
1 cup raisins
¼ cup white sugar
3 teaspoons guar gum
2 teaspoons GF active dried yeast
3 tablespoons extra light olive oil
1 teaspoon cider vinegar
350ml warm water
3 eggs

*Note: For this recipe you need a
bread-maker*

Mix the dry ingredients together in a large mixing bowl.

Beat the liquids together in a separate bowl then combine with the dry ingredients

Pour the mixture into the bread-maker loaf pan.

Push down on the mixture with a wet spatula to force out any air bubbles.

Put the bread-maker on a normal setting with a medium crust.

Remove loaf from the bread-maker as soon as it finishes baking.

Seed Bread

MAKES 1 LOAF

Mix the dry ingredients together in a large mixing bowl.

Beat the liquids together in a separate bowl then combine with the dry ingredients

Pour the mixture into the bread-maker loaf pan.

Push down on the mixture with a wet spatula to force out any air bubbles.

Put the bread-maker on a normal setting with a medium crust.

Remove loaf from the bread-maker as soon as it finishes baking.

INGREDIENTS

2 cups rice flour

½ cup maize cornflour

½ cup tapioca flour

½ cup soy flour

½ cup trim milk powder

¼ cup white sugar

3 teaspoons guar gum

2 teaspoons salt

2 teaspoons GF active dried yeast

3 tablespoons sesame seeds

3 tablespoons linseeds

2 tablespoons poppy seeds

3 tablespoons extra light olive oil

1 teaspoon cider vinegar

350ml warm water

3 eggs

Note: For this recipe you need a
    bread-maker

Focaccia Bread

MAKES 1 LOAF

INGREDIENTS

2 cups rice flour

1¾ cups soy flour

¾ cup maize cornflour

1 teaspoon sugar

1½ cups warm water

½ cup extra light olive oil

1 tablespoon GF active dried yeast

1 teaspoon salt

sprinkle of rock salt

rosemary

Mix yeast, water and sugar with electric beaters until frothy.

Sift rice flour, soy flour, maize cornflour and salt together and add oil.

Add yeast mixture to flour and mix well.

Roll dough into a ball and place in a large bowl with a damp tea-towel over it.

Place bowl in the warmest place you can find and leave for 1 hour.

Knead on floured bench and flatten into an oiled roasting dish to 2 cm thick.

Cover and rise again for 1 hour.

Make shallow grooves on the top of dough and drizzle oil over it.

Sprinkle with as much rosemary and rock salt as you want.

Bake at 180° for 15-20 minutes but it may need more.

This is best eaten straight out of the oven dipped in soup or spread with pesto and other dips.

Cheesy Cornbread

MAKES 1 LOAF

Preheat the oven to 190° and line or grease a loaf tin.

Mix cornmeal and baking powder together in a large bowl.

In a separate bowl beat eggs, oil and sour cream until smooth.

Mix the parmesan and edam cheese together and put a little aside for the top.

Pour egg mixture into dry ingredients with corn, bacon and cheese

Mix lightly until just combined.

Spoon into loaf tin and sprinkle remaining cheese on top.

Bake for 25 minutes and check with a skewer.

If ready remove from oven, otherwise leave a few minutes longer.

Cool on a wire rack.

INGREDIENTS

2 eggs
1 cup cornmeal
2 teaspoons GF baking powder
¼ cup extra light olive oil
½ cup sour cream
1 cup frozen corn
¾ cup finely chopped GF fried bacon
½ cup parmesan
1½ cups edam cheese

Mediterranean Loaf

MAKES 1 LOAF

INGREDIENTS

3 eggs
1½ cups trim milk
1¾ cups cornmeal
⅔ cup rice flour
½ teaspoon salt
4 teaspoons GF baking powder
1 tablespoon xanthan gum
1 tablespoon GF tomato paste
50g sliced black olives
50g chopped sundried tomatoes
60g grated parmesan cheese

Line a loaf tin with baking paper and preheat oven to 180°.

Sift rice flour, cornmeal, baking powder, salt and xanthan gum twice into a large bowl.

In a separate bowl beat eggs, trim milk and tomato paste till combined.

Add parmesan, sundried tomatoes and olives to the wet mixture.

Pour wet mixture into dry ingredients and mix until just combined.

Fill prepared loaf tin with the mixture.

Bake for 45 minutes or until a skewer comes out clean.

Serve warm with butter or pesto, or toasted with spreads and dips.

Corn, Cheese and Bacon Muffins

MAKES 15 MEDIUM MUFFINS OR 8 MINI LOAVES

Grease a medium muffin tin or a miniature 8 hole loaf pan.

Preheat oven to 190°.

Chop bacon into small pieces and fry then put aside.

Sift rice flour, maize cornflour, soy flour and baking powder twice into a large bowl.

Mix corn, eggs, bacon and milk together in a separate bowl.

Mix the grated edam cheese and grated parmesan cheese together.

Pour corn mixture into dry ingredients and add half the cheese.

Mix quickly until just combined.

Three-quarters fill prepared muffin tins with the mixture.

Sprinkle with remaining cheese.

Bake for 20 minutes or until muffins spring back when lightly touched.

INGREDIENTS

200g finely chopped GF bacon
1 cup rice flour
½ cup maize cornflour
½ cup soy flour
5 teaspoons GF baking powder
410g can GF cream style corn
2 eggs
1 cup trim milk
1¼ cups grated edam cheese
¾ cup grated parmesan cheese

Tomato and Olive Mini Muffins

MAKES 42 MINI MUFFIINS

INGREDIENTS

3 eggs
1 cup trim milk
¼ cup sliced black olives
6 sundried tomatoes
½ cup rice flour
¾ maize cornflour
¼ soy flour
4 teaspoons GF baking powder
1 cup grated edam cheese
¾ cup grated parmesan cheese

Grease mini muffin tin and preheat oven to 160°.

Chop sundried tomatoes finely.

Sift rice flour, maize cornflour, soy flour and baking powder twice into a large bowl.

Mix sundried tomatoes, olives, eggs and milk together in a separate bowl.

Pour wet mixture into dry ingredients.

Mix the parmesan and edam cheese and add two thirds of the cheese to the mixture.

Mix well and fill prepared muffin tin with the mixture.

Don't fill right to the top of tin.

Sprinkle remaining cheese on top of muffins.

Bake for 20 minutes.

Lemon Poppy Seed Muffins

MAKES 12

Preheat oven to 190° and grease muffin pan with butter.

Sift potato flour, soy flour, maize cornflour, rice flour, xanthan gum and baking powder together twice.

Stir poppy seeds and sugar into dry ingredients.

Melt butter, let it cool then one at a time quickly beat in trim milk, eggs then lemon juice until just combined.

Quickly combine wet and dry ingredients and fill muffin pan.

Bake for 15 minutes.

Serve warm.

3 eggs
1 cup trim milk
½ cup bottled lemon juice
100g melted butter
½ cup poppy seeds
1 teaspoon xanthan gum
3 heaped teaspoons GF baking powder
1 cup white sugar
½ cup rice flour
½ cup maize cornflour
¼ cup soy flour
¼ cup potato flour

Blueberry Muffins

MAKES 12

INGREDIENTS

3 eggs
1 cup trim milk
100g melted butter
1½ cups blueberries
1 teaspoon xanthan gum
3 heaped teaspoons GF baking powder
1 cup soft brown sugar
½ cup rice flour
½ cup maize cornflour
¼ cup soy flour
¼ cup potato flour

Preheat oven to 190° and grease muffin pan with butter.

Sift potato flour, soy flour, maize cornflour, rice flour, xanthan gum and baking powder together twice.

Stir brown sugar into dry ingredients.

Melt butter, let it cool then one at a time quickly beat in trim milk and eggs until just combined.

Pour into dry ingredients, add blueberries and fold in until just combined.

Fill muffin tin and bake for 15 minutes.

Serve warm.

Sweet Apple Mini Muffins

MAKES 48 MINI MUFFIINS

Grease mini muffin tin and preheat oven to 160°.

Chop apples into 1cm sized pieces and boil with ½ cup white sugar until soft.

Sift all remaining dry ingredients into a large mixing bowl.

Mix cooked apple, eggs, milk and vanilla essence together in a separate bowl.

Pour wet mixture into dry ingredients and combine.

Fill the muffin cavities ¾ full with the mixture.

Sprinkle the top of each mini muffin with raw sugar.

Bake for 20-25 minutes.

INGREDIENTS

¾ cup rice flour
½ cup maize cornflour
¼ cup soy flour
4 teaspoons GF baking powder
1 teaspoon mixed spice
1 teaspoon cinnamon
2 teaspoons vanilla essence
2 whole peeled apples
½ cup white sugar
½ cup soft brown sugar
1 cup trim milk
2 eggs
raw sugar to sprinkle

Apple Loaf

MAKES 1 LOAF

INGREDIENTS

50g melted butter
1 cup white sugar
1 teaspoon baking soda
⅓ cup trim milk
2 teaspoons GF baking powder
½ teaspoon mixed spice
1½ teaspoons cinnamon
½ cup soy flour
½ cup maize cornflour
1 cup rice flour
1 cup raisins
550g can GF apple pie filling
1 teaspoon vanilla essence
200g GF plain sweetened yoghurt
2 eggs

Preheat oven to 170°.

Line a large loaf tin with baking paper.

Sift rice flour, soy flour, maize cornflour, baking powder, baking soda, mixed spice and cinnamon in a large mixing bowl twice to ensure it's well mixed.

In another bowl beat sugar and eggs until thick and fluffy.

Add melted butter, trim milk, vanilla essence and yoghurt to egg mixture and beat until well combined.

Add ⅓ of the apple to the egg mixture.

Add egg mixture to flours and beat for 3 minutes.

Stir through remaining apple and raisins.

Pour into prepared loaf tin and bake at 170° for 1 hour and 10 minutes or until a skewer comes out clean.

Leave in tin for 5 minutes before lifting out and peeling off baking paper.

Serve warm with low fat spread or as a dessert with whipped cream, vanilla ice cream or hot caramel sauce.

Chocolate Cake

SERVES 8

Preheat oven to 160°.

Line a large cake tin with baking paper.

Cream butter and sugar in a large mixing bowl.

Beat in eggs, berry yoghurt, trim milk and vanilla essence one at a time.

Sift all the flours, cocoa, baking powder, baking soda and xanthan gum together two to three times to ensure they are thoroughly mixed.

Pour wet mixture into dry ingredients and fold together until combined.

Stir in chocolate chips then pour into prepared cake tin.

Bake for 1 hour but check with a skewer before removing from the oven.

Leave to cool on a wire rack before icing.

To make the icing, melt the dark cooking chocolate and butter in the microwave then beat with the sugar until cool and thick.

Spread icing on the cake and leave to set, serve with whipped cream.

INGREDIENTS

1½ cups rice flour
¾ cup soy flour
½ cup maize cornflour
¼ cup potato flour
½ cup GF cocoa powder
1 teaspoon baking soda
2 teaspoons GF baking powder
1 teaspoon xanthan gum
2 teaspoons vanilla essence
1 cup white sugar
300g GF mixed berry yoghurt
200g GF dark chocolate chips
120g unsalted butter
1½ cups trim milk
4 eggs

ICING

1 cup GF icing sugar
60g unsalted butter
120g GF dark cooking chocolate

Banana Cake

MAKES 12 PIECES

INGREDIENTS

3 eggs

130g softened butter

¾ cup white sugar

½ cup soy flour

½ cup maize cornflour

1 cup rice flour

1 teaspoon GF baking powder

1 teaspoon baking soda

2 tablespoons hot trim milk

4 medium mashed ripe bananas

Preheat oven to 180° and line a medium square cake tin with baking paper.

Sift rice flour, soy flour, maize cornflour and baking powder together twice.

In a separate bowl cream butter and sugar until light and fluffy.

Add eggs one at a time to the creamed butter, beating after each addition.

Add mashed banana to creamed mixture and mix well.

Heat milk in the microwave, add baking soda, mix quickly and add to creamed mixture.

Fold the flour into the creamed mixture until just combined.

Turn into prepared cake tin.

Bake for 40 minutes or until cake springs back when lightly touched.

Turn out onto a wire rack.

When the cake is cold slice it in half and spread mock cream through the centre, then ice with vanilla icing.

Carrot Cake

SERVES 8

Line a 8″ round cake tin and preheat oven to 160°.

Sift rice flour, soy flour, maize cornflour, baking powder, baking soda and mixed spice into a large bowl.

Stir in brown sugar, grated carrot, crushed pineapple and walnuts.

Combine oil, sour cream and eggs until smooth then mix into the other ingredients.

Pour mixture into prepared tin.

Bake for 1 hour.

When cake is cold beat the cream cheese, icing sugar and orange essence till light and fluffy and use a flat bladed knife to spread the icing over the cake.

INGREDIENTS

½ cup rice flour

½ cup soy flour

¾ cup maize cornflour

2 teaspoons GF baking powder

1 teaspoon baking soda

2 teaspoons mixed spice

1 cup packed soft brown sugar

1½ cups grated carrot

1 cup chopped walnuts

250g crushed pineapple

½ cup extra light olive oil

½ cup light sour cream

3 eggs

ORANGE CREAM CHEESE ICING

2 cups GF icing sugar

250g softened cream cheese

1 teaspoon orange essence
 (*or 2 teaspoons grated orange zest*)

Fruit Cake

MAKES 25-30 PIECES

INGREDIENTS

7 eggs

350g softened butter

1½ cups soft brown sugar

2 tablespoons golden syrup

1 cup GF plain sweetened yoghurt

1kg mixed fruit

1½ cups of rice flour

½ cup of soy flour

½ cup of potato flour

½ cup of maize cornflour

¼ cup of tapioca flour

1 tablespoon xanthan gum

3 teaspoons mixed spice

2 teaspoons GF baking powder

Line a medium sized roasting pan with baking paper and preheat oven to 150°.

In a large mixing bowl cream butter and brown sugar until light and fluffy.

Add eggs, golden syrup and plain yoghurt one at a time, beating well after each addition.

In a separate large mixing bowl sift all the flours, baking powder, mixed spice and xanthan gum together three times.

Pour wet ingredients into the dry ingredients and combine.

Add the mixed fruit and fold through.

Turn into prepared roasting pan and push cake mixture into the corners with the back of a spoon so it's evenly spread out.

Bake at 150° for 1 hour then turn oven down to 110° and cook for a further 20 minutes or until cake springs back when lightly touched.

Turn out onto a wire rack.

Apple Cake and Custard

SERVES 8

Preheat oven to 160° and line a round 8" cake tin with baking paper.

In a large mixing bowl sieve rice flour, soy flour, maize cornflour, brown sugar, baking powder, mixed spice and cinnamon twice to ensure it's well mixed.

In a separate bowl mix vanilla essence, trim milk, eggs, raisins and apple.

Pour wet ingredients into the dry ingredients and combine.

Carefully pour the mixture into the cake tin, it should fill it right to the top.

Bake for 1 hour.

Serve with custard as a dessert.

You could also serve it with vanilla ice cream or whipped cream, or put pieces of it cold into a school or work lunch.

INGREDIENTS

1 cup rice flour
½ cup soy flour
½ cup maize cornflour
4 teaspoons GF baking powder
1 cup soft brown sugar
3 teaspoons cinnamon
2 teaspoons mixed spice
2 teaspoons vanilla essence
550g tin GF apple pie filling
1 cup raisins
1 cup trim milk
2 eggs

CUSTARD

2 tablespoons GF custard powder
2 tablespoons white sugar
2 cups trim milk

Chocolate Lamingtons

MAKES 16

INGREDIENTS

4 eggs
½ cup white sugar
1 cup maize cornflour
1 teaspoon GF baking powder
40g melted butter
¾ cup boiling water
1½ teaspoons vanilla essence
2¼ cups GF icing sugar
3 tablespoons GF cocoa powder
220g desiccated coconut

Line a lamington pan or large rectangular glass dish with baking paper.

Preheat the oven to 180°.

Using an electric beater or a mixer beat the eggs until very thick and foamy.

Gradually add the sugar whilst beating, beat until shiny and all the sugar has dissolved.

Sift the cornflour and baking powder together twice then sift over the egg mixture.

Mix with a metal spoon and pour into the prepared pan or dish.

Bake for 20 minutes or until done.

Allow to cool then cut into 16 squares.

Mix together melted butter, vanilla essence, cocoa and boiling water.

Sift icing sugar over the mixture and combine.

Coat sponge squares in chocolate by dipping them into the bowl then rolling in coconut immediately.

Place on a wire rack to set, they may take a while to dry so make them in advance.

Quince Sponge Cake

SERVES 8

Line two 8″ cake tins with baking paper and preheat the oven to 180°.

Using an electric beater beat the eggs until very thick and foamy.

Gradually add the sugar whilst beating, beat until shiny and all the sugar has dissolved.

Sift the maize cornflour and baking powder together twice then sift over the egg mixture.

Mix with a metal spoon and pour into the two prepared cake tins.

Bake for 20 minutes or until done.

Leave for 5 minutes before removing from the tins and peeling the paper off.

Once completely cool spread one side of a sponge with quince jelly, whip the cream with icing sugar and vanilla essence then spread over the quince jelly.

Place the top half of the sponge on the cream and dust the top of the sponge with icing sugar using a sieve.

Consume on the same day as making.

INGREDIENTS

1 cup maize cornflour

1 teaspoon GF baking powder

½ cup white sugar

4 eggs

2 cups cream

¼ cup quince jelly

¼ cup GF icing sugar

1 teaspoon vanilla essence

Icing and Fillings

CHOCOLATE ICING

2 cups GF icing sugar
2 tablespoons GF cocoa
2 tablespoons water
¼ teaspoon butter
1 teaspoon vanilla essence

Sift icing sugar and cocoa into a bowl.

Add butter, vanilla essence and water.

Add enough extra water to mix to a spreadable consistency.

VANILLA ICING

2 cups GF icing sugar
2 tablespoons water
¼ teaspoon butter
1 teaspoon vanilla essence

Sift GF icing sugar into a bowl.

Add butter, vanilla essence and water.

Add enough extra water to mix to a spreadable consistency.

LEMON ICING

2 cups GF icing sugar
2 tablespoons lemon juice
¼ teaspoon butter

Sift icing sugar into a bowl.

Add butter and lemon juice.

Add enough water to mix to a spreadable consistency.

ORANGE CREAM CHEESE ICING

2 cups GF icing sugar
250g softened cream cheese
1 teaspoon orange essence (or 2 teaspoons grated orange zest)

Beat cream cheese, icing sugar and orange essence till light and fluffy.

MOCK CREAM

1 cup GF icing sugar
100g softened butter
1 tablespoon milk
1 teaspoon of vanilla essence

Cream butter and sugar until light and fluffy.

Add milk and vanilla essence.

Beat until thick and pale like cream.

BUTTER ICING

2 cups GF icing sugar
100g softened butter
1 teaspoon vanilla essence
2 tablespoons hot water

Cream butter until light and fluffy.

Add vanilla essence.

Add sugar and beat into butter.

Add enough water to mix to a spreadable consistency.

Melting Moments

MAKES 48 BISCUITS

Cover an oven tray with baking paper and preheat oven to 180°.

Cream butter and icing sugar until light and fluffy.

Sift maize cornflour, rice flour, soy flour, potato flour, baking powder and xanthan gum.

Add to butter and icing sugar and mix well.

Roll dough into balls roughly 2cm in diameter and place on prepared oven tray.

Press down slightly with a fork on each one.

Bake for 10 to 15 minutes but watch closely as this varies.

Cool biscuits for at least 10 minutes before moving from the tray.

When cold sandwich two biscuits together with vanilla icing, lemon icing, raspberry jam, or eat them plain.

INGREDIENTS

200g softened butter

¾ cup GF icing sugar

1 cup maize cornflour

½ cup rice flour

¼ cup soy flour

¼ cup potato flour

1 teaspoon GF baking powder

1 tablespoon xanthan gum

Nan's Highlander Square

MAKES 20-25 PIECES

INGREDIENTS

BASE

170g unsalted butter
3 tablespoons sugar
1 teaspoon vanilla essence
1 teaspoon GF baking powder
1¾ cups tapioca flour

CARAMEL

60g butter
2 tablespoons golden syrup
1 teaspoon vanilla essence
200g sweetened condensed milk

Preheat the oven to 190°.

Line a glass or metal square baking dish with baking paper.

Cream the butter and sugar for the base and mix in the vanilla essence.

Add tapioca flour and baking powder and mix well with an electric beater.

If the mixture is sticky add more flour until it's smooth and able to be rolled into a ball.

Press most of the mixture firmly into the lined dish, leaving just enough to crumble over the top later.

Heat condensed milk, butter, golden syrup and vanilla essence in a saucepan until the butter is melted and the ingredients are blended.

Remove from the heat then pour caramel onto the base.

Disperse the remaining base mixture over the top of the caramel, if it is clumped together, add more tapioca flour, beat with the electric beaters and it will become more crumbly.

Bake for 20 to 30 minutes until the caramel is brown and bubbling.

Leave to cool fully before removing from the baking dish as it will fall apart until its cold.

This square is very rich and meant as a treat so is best kept sliced into small pieces and kept in the fridge in a sealed container.

Chocolate Raisin Slice

MAKES 15-20 PIECES

Line a glass or metal rectangular baking dish with baking paper.

Crush biscuits and add raisins, drinking chocolate powder and butter then mix well.

Press mixture firmly into lined dish and refrigerate.

Heat condensed milk in a saucepan with 2 teaspoons of margarine and golden syrup on a low heat for five minutes stirring all the time until it turns light brown.

Pour the caramel over the base and set aside.

Melt dark cooking chocolate and the remaining margarine in the microwave.

When fully melted pour over caramel and spread to the edges with the back of a metal spoon.

Refrigerate for two hours.

Slice into small squares.

INGREDIENTS

200g GF plain sweet biscuits

120g melted unsalted butter

2 heaped tablespoons GF drinking chocolate powder

¾ cup of raisins

200g GF dark cooking chocolate

4 teaspoons margarine

1 tablespoon golden syrup

395g can sweetened condensed milk

Peanut Chocolate Truffles

MAKES 50 TRUFFLES

INGREDIENTS

100g butter
½ cup GF peanut butter
1 cup GF plain sweet biscuits
1 cup GF icing sugar
1 teaspoon vanilla essence
200g GF dark chocolate
200g GF white chocolate

In a large bowl melt peanut butter and butter in the microwave then stir until smooth.

Use the food processor to crush the biscuits into fine crumbs.

Stir in biscuit crumbs, vanilla essence and icing sugar.

Break mixture up and roll into balls about the size of large marbles.

Melt the dark chocolate in the microwave.

Dip balls using a teaspoon to coat them fully, then lay them on baking paper to set.

Melt the white chocolate in the microwave and pick up each ball and dip them to coat the top half , then lay back on the baking paper white side up.

You could dip them in crushed nuts such as pistachios, drizzle dark chocolate over them to decorate (as pictured) or leave as they are.

Store in the freezer in a sealed container.

Rice Puff Crunch

MAKES 15 PIECES

Lay out a sheet of baking paper on the bench.

Boil butter, sugar and honey for 5-10 minutes until golden brown and bubbly.

Mix in rice puffs till combined and turn out onto the baking paper.

Press the rice puffs flat to a 2cm thickness with the back of a spoon.

Allow to cool then cut into slices.

Store in a sealed container.

INGREDIENTS

100g butter
80g sugar
2 heaped tablespoons honey
3 cups GF rice puffs/bubbles

Rice Puff Crunch Deluxe

MAKES 15 PIECES

INGREDIENTS

100g butter
80g sugar
2 heaped tablespoons honey
80g GF chocolate chips
10 GF marshmallows
3 cups GF rice puffs/bubbles.

Lay out a sheet of baking paper on the bench.

Boil butter, sugar and honey for 5-10 minutes until golden brown and bubbly.

Mix in rice puffs till combined then mix in the chocolate chips and marshmallows.

Turn out onto the baking paper.

Press the rice puffs flat to a 2cm thickness with the back of a spoon.

Allow to cool then cut into slices.

Store in a sealed container.

Desserts

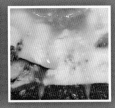

Pineapple Crunch Pudding

SERVES 8

INGREDIENTS

300g GF vanilla ice cream
70g GF vanilla instant dessert powder
500ml trim milk
¼ cup soft brown sugar
120g melted unsalted butter
200g crushed GF cornflakes
1/3 cup boiling water
3 tablespoons gelatine
1½ cups crushed pineapple
1-2 cups GF pineapple jelly

Line a 8" round cake tin with plastic wrap (one with high sides is best).

Use a food processor to crush cornflakes until they are mostly fine crumbs.

Mix the cornflakes with melted butter and brown sugar and when the mixture has cooled press firmly into the bottom of the tin with the back of a metal spoon.

Place tin in the fridge while you prepare the next stage.

Combine boiling water and gelatine in a heat-proof jug.

Set jug in a larger pot of water and simmer gently on the stove, stirring until the gelatine is dissolved then set aside to cool.

Beat the trim milk and vanilla dessert powder well so no lumps remain.

Measure out the ice cream and using the electric hand mixer, combine the instant dessert and ice cream until smooth.

Once the gelatine has completely cooled but is still liquid, add to the mixture and beat in with the hand mixer.

Pour the vanilla mixture into the tin and return it the fridge to set.

One hour later mix up the pineapple jelly and leave to cool.

When the pineapple jelly is cold but not set pour over the vanilla mixture.

Spoon the crushed pineapple over the top of the dessert and return it to the fridge to set for at least 2 hours before serving.

Hokey Pokey Cheesecake

SERVES 8

Line 8" round cake tin with plastic wrap.

Blend biscuits, icing sugar and cocoa in food processor then mix with melted butter and after it has cooled press into tin.

In a small pot make caramel sauce by melting brown sugar, 20g butter and 3 tablespoons of cream on low heat and put to the side to cool.

Put the ¼ cup water in a heatproof jug and sprinkle gelatine over the top.

Stand the jug in a pot of simmering water and stir gelatine until dissolved then remove the jug from the pot and stand to cool.

Using electric beaters mix softened cream cheese and white sugar in a large bowl until smooth.

Whip the rest of the cream with icing sugar and set aside.

Break and crumble the hokey pokey into pieces then mix gelatine and hokey pokey into the cream cheese mixture.

Fold whipped cream into the cream cheese mixture.

Pour the cream cheese mixture onto the base

Smooth the top of the cheesecake using a spatula.

Pour the caramel on last as the topping.

Refrigerate for at least 3 hours before serving.

INGREDIENTS

½ cup soft brown sugar

½ cup white sugar

½ cup GF icing sugar

20g butter

¼ cup water

3 heaped teaspoons gelatine

500g softened cream cheese

300ml cream

2 GF hokey pokey chocolate bars

BASE

100g melted unsalted butter

2 heaped tablespoons GF icing sugar

2 heaped tablespoons GF cocoa powder

200g GF plain sweet biscuits

Mint Chocolate Cheesecake

SERVES 8

INGREDIENTS

150g GF white chocolate
½ cup boiling water
1 tablespoon gelatine
500g cream cheese
395g can sweetened condensed milk
1 teaspoon peppermint essence
5 drops green food colouring
50g GF dark cooking chocolate

BASE

200g GF plain sweet biscuits
2 tablespoons GF cocoa powder
2 tablespoons GF icing sugar
80g melted butter

Line a round 8" cake tin with plastic wrap.

Crush biscuits, add melted butter, icing sugar and cocoa and mix well.

Press firmly onto the base of the tin and smooth with the back of a spoon.

Combine boiling water and gelatine in a heat-proof jug.

Set jug in a larger pot of water and simmer gently on the stove until gelatine is dissolved then set aside to cool.

Break up and melt white chocolate in a microwave safe bowl and set aside to cool.

Combine cream cheese, sweetened condensed milk, white chocolate, peppermint essence and dissolved gelatine in a food processor and mix until smooth.

Pour half the mixture into a mixing bowl and add the green food colouring then mix well.

Pour the remainder of the mixture into the mixing bowl and stir it briefly so it creates a swirly marbled pattern then pour onto the biscuit base

Melt dark cooking chocolate in the microwave for a minute and spread over a sheet of baking paper.

When the chocolate is dried use a sharp knife to shave bits off to make decorations for the top of the cheesecake.

Refrigerate for at least 2 hours before serving and you can make it the day before if that's more convenient.

White Chocolate Mousse

SERVES 2

Whip cream with caster sugar until it forms soft peaks.

Melt white chocolate in a pot balanced over another of boiling water (known as double boiling) or microwave it.

Leave chocolate to cool then before its set mix in one third of the cream.

When the cream and chocolate are well combined, fold in the remainder of the cream and refrigerate.

Dissolve white sugar and ½ cup of water in a pot.

Bring to the boil then reduce the heat and simmer until golden and caramelized.

Drizzle toffee in patterns over baking paper wrapped over the bottom of 4 teacups and leave to harden.

Turn upside down, peel off baking paper and set aside.

You can also make shapes out of the toffee using metal cookie cutters.

Simply sit the shape over a sheet of baking paper, fill with a thin layer of the toffee and don't move it until it has fully set, you'll then be able to pop the toffee shape out of the metal mould easily.

Leave mousse in the fridge to set for at least two hours before serving.

To serve the mousse spoon into toffee baskets and decorate with toffee shapes and fragments.

INGREDIENTS

1 cup cream
80g good quality GF white chocolate
¼ cup caster sugar
1 cup white sugar
½ cup water

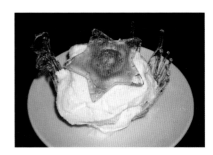

Strawberry Meringues

MAKES 24

INGREDIENTS

6 egg whites at room temperature

2 cups white sugar

1 teaspoon white vinegar

2 teaspoons maize cornflour

2 teaspoons vanilla essence

400ml cream

½ cup GF icing sugar

1 punnet of fresh strawberries or 1 tin of drained strawberries

Preheat oven to 120°.

Beat egg whites in a large mixing bowl until soft peaks form.

Add the white sugar to the egg whites slowly over 10 minutes beating constantly.

Mix white vinegar, maize cornflour and vanilla essence together until all lumps are gone.

Add to the meringue mixture and beat in well.

Cover an oven tray in baking paper and spoon the meringues onto the paper.

Bake for 45 minutes then remove to cool.

Chop the strawberries up finely then add to the cream.

Whip the cream, icing sugar and strawberries together.

Just before serving the meringues spoon generous amounts of strawberry cream onto them and arrange on a large platter.

Mango Pavlova

SERVES 8

Preheat oven to 180°.

Beat egg whites and white sugar for 10 minutes or until thick and shiny.

Mix white vinegar, maize cornflour and two teaspoons of vanilla essence in a separate bowl.

Mix liquid into the meringue and beat for a few minutes.

Cover an oven tray in baking paper and spread the pavlova into a round shape about 20cm in diameter.

Use a spatula or knife to smooth the sides and top of the meringue.

Place pavlova in preheated oven and turn temperature down to 100°.

Leave for 50 minutes to 1 hour then remove to cool.

Whip the cream, icing sugar and 2 teaspoons of vanilla essence and spread over top of pavlova.

Puree the mango slices to make a sauce and drizzle over the pavlova.

Decorate with halved strawberries.

INGREDIENTS

4 egg whites at room temperature

1½ cups white sugar

1 teaspoon white vinegar

1 tablespoon maize cornflour

4 teaspoons vanilla essence

400ml cream

½ cup GF icing sugar

1 punnet of strawberries

425g can mango slices

Crème Caramel

SERVES 6

INGREDIENTS

1 cup sugar

⅓ cup caster sugar

3 cups trim milk

4 eggs

2 teaspoons vanilla essence

Grease a loaf tin and preheat oven to 160°.

Dissolve sugar and ½ cup of water in a pot.

Bring to the boil then reduce the heat and simmer until golden and caramelized.

Remove from heat quickly and pour into loaf tin.

Heat the trim milk on low heat until almost boiling.

While trim milk is heating beat eggs, caster sugar and vanilla essence for 2 minutes.

Add the hot milk to the egg mixture and strain into a jug.

Pour the mixture into the loaf tin.

Place the loaf tin in the centre of a roasting pan and fill pan with boiling water at least halfway up the side of loaf tin.

Bake for 30 minutes.

Allow to cool then place in fridge for 2 hours before serving.

When serving run a dinner knife lightly around the edge of the crème caramel and upturn onto a large rectangular dish with a dip so the caramel sauce can pool.

Using the blunt end of the dinner knife crack and splinter the remaining caramel that has hardened onto the bottom of the tin and use it to decorate the crème caramel.

Banoffee Pie

SERVES 8

Line an 8" cake tin with plastic wrap.

Crush biscuits in the food processor.

Mix ginger powder, mixed spice, icing sugar and crushed biscuits together.

Melt the butter and mix into the biscuit crumbs, wait for it to cool but before it sets press biscuit mixture onto the bottom of the tin, smooth and press down with the back of a spoon.

Put ½ cup water in a heatproof jug and sprinkle gelatine over the top.

Stand the jug in a pot of simmering water and stir gelatine until dissolved then remove jug and stand to cool.

Whip cream and put aside.

Heat condensed milk, golden syrup and margarine until it turns pale brown and looks like caramel, remove from the heat and cool quickly by sitting the pot in cold water in the sink.

When the gelatine is cold but not set fold it into the cold caramel and mix well.

Combine the whipped cream and caramel and pour over the biscuit base.

Drizzle chocolate sauce or melted chocolate in a spiral over cream mixture.

Using a kebab skewer drag it through the mixture to create a marbled effect.

Refrigerate for 3 hours.

Serve with sliced banana piled on top or in a ring around the top edge of the pie.

INGREDIENTS

395g can sweetened condensed milk
2 tablespoons golden syrup
1 teaspoon margarine
2 sliced bananas
250ml cream
1 kebab skewer
½ cup water
1 tablespoon gelatine
2 tablespoons GF thick chocolate sauce
(*or you can use melted GF dark chocolate*)

BASE

200g GF plain sweet biscuits
2 tablespoons GF icing sugar
3 teaspoons ginger powder
1½ teaspoons mixed spice
100g melted unsalted butter

Custard Pie

SERVES 8

INGREDIENTS

½ cup GF custard powder
½ cup rice flour
½ cup maize cornflour
¼ cup soy flour
125g chilled chopped butter
4 tablespoons white sugar
1 egg yolk
½ teaspoon nutmeg

CUSTARD

4 tablespoons GF custard powder
4 tablespoons white sugar
4 cups trim milk
3 teaspoons gelatine

Line a 8" glass, metal or ceramic deep round baking dish with baking paper folding it over the edges of the dish.

Sift rice flour, maize cornflour, soy flour and custard powder into a bowl.

Using your fingers rub the butter into the mix until it resembles breadcrumbs.

Stir in sugar then use a flat bladed knife to mix in yolk and two tablespoons of water to make dough.

Roll the soft dough into a ball, wrap in plastic and place in fridge for 30 minutes.

Preheat oven to 190°.

Roll pastry out between two sheets of baking paper then line the base and sides of the dish with the pastry.

Line the dish with baking paper over the pastry and fill with baking beads or rice then bake for 20 minutes.

Remove the paper and beads/rice and bake for a further 5-10 minutes.

Combine custard powder, sugar, gelatine and 1 cup of trim milk in a large bowl.

Stir the remaining milk into the custard mixture and microwave on high for 10 minutes, stirring every two minutes (you can make the custard the traditional way if you prefer).

When the custard has cooled but not set (about 20 minutes) pour it into the pastry case, sprinkle with nutmeg and refrigerate for 3 hours.

When ready to serve lift pie out of the dish and peel off baking paper.

Serve with fruit salad.

Apple Pie

SERVES 4

Preheat oven to 180°.

Sift flours and custard powder into a large bowl.

Rub in the butter until the mixture resembles breadcrumbs.

Stir in the sugar and use a flat bladed knife to mix in yolk and water to form a soft dough.

Roll into a ball, wrap in plastic and put in the fridge for 30 minutes.

Mix apples, raisins and brown sugar and put in a round 8" ceramic dish or something similar

Roll out dough between 2 sheets of baking paper and cut a circle to fit over the apple mixture.

Use the leftovers to cut out leaf shapes for the top of the pie.

Brush top with a small amount of milk and brown sugar.

Bake for 25 - 30 minutes.

Serve on its own, with whipped cream or vanilla ice cream.

INGREDIENTS

1 egg yolk
2 tablespoons white sugar
½ cup GF custard powder
2 tablespoons water
110g butter
¼ cup soy flour
¼ cup rice flour
½ cup maize cornflour
½ cup raisins
¼ cup soft brown sugar
550g can GF apple pie filling
extra brown sugar and milk to glaze

Apple Crumble

SERVES 4

INGREDIENTS

¾ cup rice flour
70g softened butter
½ cup soft brown sugar
3 tablespoons desiccated coconut
550g can GF apple pie filling

Preheat oven to 180°.

Put apple pie filling into a 8" ceramic dish or something similar.

In a medium mixing bowl stir coconut, brown sugar and rice flour together.

Rub the butter into the dry mixture using your fingertips until it resembles crumbs or use a food processor to blend it all together.

Sprinkle the mixture over the apple and place in oven.

Bake for 30 minutes.

Serve on its own, with whipped cream, ice cream or custard.

Sticky Date Pudding

SERVES 8

Preheat oven to 180°.

Line a 8″ round cake tin with baking paper.

Combine dates, boiling water and baking soda in a mixing bowl.

Stand date mixture for 5 minutes then add margarine and brown sugar.

Mix in a food processor until smooth then add the eggs.

Sieve the flours and baking powder together three times then add to the food processor and mix until just combined.

Pour mixture into cake tin and bake for 45 minutes or until cooked through.

To make the caramel sauce combine and melt the ingredients in a pot stirring over low heat until it's dissolved.

Serve with vanilla ice cream on the side.

INGREDIENTS

1¼ cups chopped pitted dates
1¼ cups boiling water
1 teaspoon baking soda
1 teaspoon GF baking powder
½ cup maize cornflour
¼ cup rice flour
¼ cup soy flour
60g margarine
¾ cup soft brown sugar
2 eggs

CARAMEL SAUCE

2 cups soft brown sugar
50g margarine
1 teaspoon vanilla essence
250ml cream

Coconut Rice Pudding

SERVES 4

INGREDIENTS

5 tablespoons short grain white rice

400ml can light coconut milk

1 cup trim milk

1 teaspoon vanilla essence

1 teaspoon margarine

3 tablespoons white sugar

425g can mango slices

Preheat oven to 150°.

Mix sugar, vanilla essence, coconut milk, trim milk, margarine and rice in a 8" round ceramic dish or something similar.

Bake for an hour and a half stirring three times during the first hour.

Serve warm with mango slices.

Raspberry Trifle

SERVES 8-10

Mix the raspberry jelly with the boiling water and extra gelatine in a large shallow rectangular glass dish (you will need to do this the night before so it has time to set).

Line two 8" cake tins with baking paper and preheat the oven to 180°.

Using an electric beater beat the eggs until thick and foamy.

Gradually add the sugar whilst beating, beat until shiny and all the sugar has dissolved.

Sift the maize cornflour and baking powder together twice then sift over the egg mixture.

Mix with a metal spoon and pour into the two prepared cake tins.

Bake for 20 minutes or until done.

Leave for 5 minutes before removing from the tins and peeling the paper off.

Allow to cool then cut into cubes about 1-2 inches.

Lay pieces of sponge around the bottom of a large glass serving bowl.

Drain the peaches and mix 1 cup of sherry with the syrup.

Layer the peaches over the sponge in the bowl.

Pour ½ the sherry and syrup mixture over the sponge and peaches.

Pour ⅓ of the custard over the sponge and peaches.

When the jelly is set cut it into cubes like the sponge and layer it in the bowl.

Add another layer of sponge, the remainder of the sherry and syrup mix and the rest of the custard.

Whip the cream with icing sugar and vanilla essence then layer over the custard.

Break up the chocolate flakes and sprinkle over the top.

INGREDIENTS

250ml cream
2 tablespoons GF icing sugar
1 teaspoon vanilla essence
2 packets GF raspberry jelly
4 cups boiling water
1 teaspoon gelatine (optional)
1 GF chocolate flake bar
1kg GF pre-made runny custard
1 can diced peaches in syrup
1 cup sherry
1 cup maize cornflour
1 teaspoon GF baking powder
½ cup white sugar
4 eggs

Notes